Saint Bernard

Saint Bernard Care & Information Guide

Saint Bernard Characteristics, Personality and
Temperament, Diet, Health, Where to Buy, Cost,
Rescue and Adoption, Care and Grooming,
Training, Breeding, and Much More Included!

By Lolly Brown

Copyrights and Trademarks

Disclaimer and Legal Notice

Foreword

If you've seen the movie Beethoven, you've probably fallen in love with the main character, just like how the rest of the world did. Beethoven (the dog) is a Saint Bernard, and in popular culture, the Saint Bernard is depicted as a huge, fluffy dog with a small barrel of brandy around its neck. The breed is known to help find and save lost and injured travelers stranded in the snow of the Alps. The Saint Bernard is a gentle giant, with its kind, calm and intelligent nature, which makes the breed a popular choice for families. No wonder it's very popular in family movies and series like the 1972 show George and of course, the 1992 movie Beethoven.

Want to take care of your own Saint Bernard? Find out everything you need to know about the breed here, from bathing to training techniques to the habitat requirement and the feeding dos and don'ts. So turn that page and get ready to get to know your new best friend!

Table of Contents

Introduction

In a popular quote, Josh Billings said, *"A dog is the only thing on Earth that loves you more than you love yourself."* There is no better feeling than coming home from a long day at work and being greeted by your pet dog. But before you can get your very own canine companion, it's best you do some research to find out which breed suits you best. Take into consideration your lifestyle, first and foremost, as well as your personality. Do you love exploring outdoors? Are you into athletic sports? Would you rather have a quiet night at home?

Once you know all the answers to those questions, it's time to look into the dog breed that is right for you.

In this book, you will learn about the Saint Bernard. This particular breed takes pride in its calm, sweet behavior, great for indoor-loving folks looking for a loyal and adorable companion. Known for being the rescuers of the Alps, this dog breed is one of the best family companions, childhood playmates and guardians you can hope for. Before you decide on getting your very own Saint Bernard, read the next couple of pages to see if this breed is indeed for you!

Glossary of Dog Terms

AKC – American Kennel Club, the largest purebred dog registry in the United States

Almond Eye – Referring to an elongated eye shape rather than a rounded shape

Apple Head – A round-shaped skull

Balance – A show term referring to all of the parts of the dog, both moving and standing, which produce a harmonious image

Beard – Long, thick hair on the dog's underjaw

Best in Show – An award given to the only undefeated dog left standing at the end of judging

Bitch – A female dog

Bite – The position of the upper and lower teeth when the dog's jaws are closed; positions include level, undershot, scissors, or overshot

Blaze – A white stripe running down the center of the face between the eyes

Board – To house, feed, and care for a dog for a fee

Breed – A domestic race of dogs having a common gene pool and characterized appearance/function

Breed Standard – A published document describing the look, movement, and behavior of the perfect specimen of a particular breed

Buff – off-white to gold coloring

Clip – A method of trimming the coat in some breeds

Coat – The hair covering of a dog; some breeds have two coats, and outer coat and undercoat; also known as a double coat. Examples of breeds with double coats include German Shepherd, Siberian Husky, Akita, etc.

Condition – The health of the dog as shown by its skin, coat, behavior, and general appearance

Crate – A container used to house and transport dogs; also called a cage or kennel

Crossbreed (Hybrid) – A dog having a sire and dam of two different breeds; cannot be registered with the AKC

Dam (bitch) – The female parent of a dog;

Dock – To shorten the tail of a dog by surgically removing the end part of the tail.

Double Coat – Having an outer weather-resistant coat and a soft, waterproof coat for warmth; see above.

Drop Ear – An ear in which the tip of the ear folds over and hangs down; not prick or erect

Entropion – A genetic disorder resulting in the upper or lower eyelid turning in

Fancier – A person who is especially interested in a particular breed or dog sport

Fawn – A red-yellow hue of brown

Feathering – A long fringe of hair on the ears, tail, legs, or body of a dog

Groom – To brush, trim, comb or otherwise make a dog's coat neat in appearance

Heel – To command a dog to stay close by its owner's side

Hip Dysplasia – A condition characterized by the abnormal formation of the hip joint

Inbreeding – The breeding of two closely related dogs of one breed

Kennel – A building or enclosure where dogs are kept

Litter – A group of puppies born at one time

Markings – A contrasting color or pattern on a dog's coat

Mask – Dark shading on the dog's foreface

Mate – To breed a dog and a bitch

Neuter – To castrate a male dog or spay a female dog

Pads – The tough, shock-absorbent skin on the bottom of a dog's foot

Parti-Color – A coloration of a dog's coat consisting of two or more definite, well-broken colors; one of the colors must be white

Pedigree – The written record of a dog's genealogy going back three generations or more

Pied – A coloration on a dog consisting of patches of white and another color

Prick Ear – Ear that is carried erect, usually pointed at the tip of the ear

Puppy – A dog under 12 months of age

Purebred – A dog whose sire and dam belong to the same breed and who are of unmixed descent

Saddle – Colored markings in the shape of a saddle over the back; colors may vary

Shedding – The natural process whereby old hair falls off the dog's body as it is replaced by new hair growth.

Sire – The male parent of a dog

Smooth Coat – Short hair that is close-lying

Spay – The surgery to remove a female dog's ovaries, rendering her incapable of breeding

Trim – To groom a dog's coat by plucking or clipping

Undercoat – The soft, short coat typically concealed by a longer outer coat

Wean – The process through which puppies transition from subsisting on their mother's milk to eating solid food

Whelping – The act of birthing a litter of puppies

Chapter One: The Saint Bernard Breed

The Saint Bernard is known around the world for its heroism, with it saving thousands of stranded travelers in the Alps. But since the availability of several modes of transportations, the Saint Bernard is now known as a gentle companion and a wonderful show dog.

In this chapter, you will learn about the history of the Saint Bernard, its physical characteristics, and a whole lot more. Hopefully with all these pieces of information, you would be able to know if this breed is indeed compatible to you.

Facts about Saint Bernard

Saint Bernard dogs are natural born trailblazers with a very impressive sense of smell. They have a natural instinct to seek out people, which helps them detect persons who are buried up to 20 feet in snow. They have huge paws that allow them to dig, and walk in snow without slipping. On the one hand, Saint Bernard do drool a lot because of the shape of their jaws – you will immediately notice the loose skin around the facial area.

The average weight of the breed is between 110 to 200 pounds, and the height is approximately 25.5 to 27.5 inches. The Saint Bernard can either have a smooth or rough coat, with the color varying from brindle grizzle, brown and white, mahogany and white, orange and white, red and white, rust and white, white and brown, white orange, and white and red. Both types of coat are easy to groom, all you need is a comb and brush with firm bristles. You only need to bathe when absolutely necessary, because shampoo may strip the coat of its oily, water-resistant properties. The Saint Bernard also has a distinct black mask marking. The breed is noticeably tall, with a very intelligent expression. It has a powerful head and is very strong and muscular in every part.

The breed is considerably calm indoors, but it would be ideal if you have a yard that he can access so he has room to spread out. He can also live in small quarters but has to be taken to regular daily walks. Long walks are also ideal to keep your Saint Bernard in good mental and physical condition. Saint Bernard puppies cannot get too much exercise, at least until their bones are already well-formed and strong enough to support strenuous activities. If you can tolerate a mess, you would most likely do well with a Saint Bernard.

When it comes to companionship, the Saint Bernard isn't suited to live indoors with very little human companionship and interaction. They work best with families and kids – they are very patient and gentle with kids and will bark only if there is cause. They have great protective instincts that can help them keep you and your family safe from any home intruder. Saint Bernard are extremely loyal and very willing to please. You will not have any problem training the breed as well – they are very intelligent, but training has to start very early. Make sure you teach them not to jump on people early on, because with their size, you would surely have very unhappy guests if your Saint Bernard jumps on them.

Saint Bernard doesn't do well in hot weathers, warm rooms and cars and because of their size; they have a shorter-than-average canine life span. The breed is also probe to health problems like the "wobbler" syndrome, which is a disease of the cervical spine, common in large and giant-breed dogs. Your Saint Bernard is also at risk of getting heart complications, skin problems, hip dysplasia, tumors and twisted stomachs. The common life expectancy of a Saint Bernard is about 8-10 years.

Summary of Saint Bernard Facts

Pedigree: originated in Switzerland

AKC Group: Mastiff, AKC Working

Breed Size: Large

Height: average 25.5 – 27.5 inches

Weight: 110 – 200 pounds

Coat Length: can have either long or short hair

Coat Texture: fine and smooth

Shedding: sheds twice a year (during spring and fall)

Color: brindle grizzle, brown and white, mahogany and white, orange and white, red and white, rust and white, white and brown, white orange, white and red

Eyes: medium-sized set to the sides, and dark in color

Nose: broad, with wide-open nostrils, black

Ears: medium-sized ears that are set high, dropping, and slightly away from the head

Tail: long, broad and powerful at the base, often held low when the dog is relaxed

Temperament: gentle, friendly, slow, patient, obedient, loyal

Strangers: generally friendly to everyone

Children: generally good with children, but (like all dogs) should be supervised around young and small children

Other Dogs: generally good with other dogs and other animals if properly trained and socialized

Training: very easy to train

Exercise Needs: needs to be exercised regularly, with long walks and short games

Health Conditions: hip dysplasia, allergies, hemi vertebrae, IDD, Elongated Soft Palate

Lifespan: 8 – 10 years

Nickname: Saint

Saint Bernard Breed History

Since the 18th century, monks living along the dangerous Saint Bernard Pass kept Saint Bernard to help them rescue stranded travelers after a bad snowstorm. The snowy Saint Bernard Pass is a route through the Alps between Italy and Switzerland. Thanks to the Saint Bernard's amazing sense of direction and resistance to the cold, over 2,000 people have been rescued from this perilous path.

Around the year 1050, the Augustine Monk St. Bernard de Menthon founded a hospice and monastery that helps struggling trekkers through the 49-mile Western Alps route. The monks at the hospice acquired their first Saint Bernard, which were descendants of the mastiff-style Asiatic dogs from the Romans. The first canines served as watchdogs and companions – they were considerably smaller in size, with shorter reddish brown and white fur, and a longer tail.

In the next 150 years, Saint Bernard has been known to find buried travelers, dig through the snow and provide warmth to the injured. Although the breed is often depicted in pop culture with a small barrel around its neck, no historical record has offered proof that the Saint Bernard did carry those flasks during rescue missions.

Chapter Two: General Requirements for Saint Bernard

Owning a Saint Bernard is not all fun and cute: taking care of these puppies or dogs cost a considerable measure. In this section you will discover exactly what you have to know before setting out on the trip of being a legitimate dog owner. This part ought to help you advance in making an informed decision on whether you are capable and prepared to possess a pet like the Saint Bernard.

Dog Licenses

Before getting a Saint Bernard, you must find out about certain licensing needs which can benefit you and your dog. The licensing needs for dog owners vary from one country to another which means you need to do a little bit of research on your own to figure out whether you wish to get a dog license or not. Within the United States, there are no federal requirements for dog licensing, however it's determined at the state level. Whereas some states don't, most states need dog homeowners to license their dogs on an annual basis.

Licensing Your Dog in United States

Even if your state doesn't require you to license your dog it is still a good idea because it will help someone to identify him if he gets lost so they can return him to you. Dog licenses in the United States usually cost approximately $25 per year and they can be renewed annually when you renew your dog's rabies vaccine.

Dog license will serve as your tracker so make sure that the documents are updated when you apply for a dog license this will also serve as a proof that your dog has been given a rabies vaccine.

Licensing Your Dog in Europe

The cost to license your dog in the U.K. is similar to the U.S. which is more or less £20, but you do not have to have your dog vaccinated against rabies. In the United Kingdom, licensing requirements for dog owners are a little bit different and it is imposed. In Europe, particularly in Great Britain, they require that all dog owners license their dogs and get it renewed every twelve months or annually. The reason for this is because rabies does not exist in the U.K. anymore, it was eradicated a long time ago, through careful control measures. If you travel with your dog to or from the U.K., you will have to obtain a special animal moving license and your dog may have to undergo a period of quarantine to make sure he doesn't carry disease into the country.

Do Saint Bernard Breeds Get Along with Other Pets?

The answer to this is both yes and no. If a Saint Bernard is successfully trained and adequately socialized – then yes, he will definitely get along well with other pets. Saint Bernard is generally very friendly towards all kinds of animals and even with strangers. However, if these dogs are spoiled too much by their owner, they can sometimes become territorial and jealous of other pets going near or getting any attention from their owner. If you don't socialize them at an early age, and teach them certain boundaries – then no they may not get along with other pets and could also be aggressive towards people.

How Many Saint Bernard Dogs Should You Keep?

It actually depends on you on how many can you take care of. If you are an experienced dog owner or just simply love the company of dogs, then you might want to consider getting another one of this breed, having more than one Saint Bernard means that you'll have no shortage of entertainment and affection. Take into consideration that these dogs thrive on being the center of attention and jealousy can become a problem. The chance of dealing with quarreling for attention amongst them is highly possible. If you do decide to get more than one, make sure you don't play favorites because it might cause emotional damage to the less favored one/s.

On the other hand, if you are a first time dog owner, it might be best to see for yourself if you can handle more than one, Saint Bernard are high maintenance dogs that needs to be trained, you must give them your full attention, if you are inexperienced, then it is highly recommended that you settle with one dog first and learn from it so that if ever you decide to get another one in the future, you'll be well-equip and knowledgeable already.

General Cost in Keeping a Saint Bernard

Owning a dog or any pet in general is not always about the cuteness or the glamour, it comes with hard work and of course the financial capacity of your wallet. Owning pets mean including them in your budget because the expenses are as a regular as your grocery and utility bills. Basically if you own a dog, it's like you've adopted a baby, you need to nurture it and take care of all its needs to keep it healthy and happy. Spending money on your Saint Bernard will begin even before you take him home because you have to prepare for his arrival and you have to purchase a crate, toys, indoor gates or fences, and food bowls. The responsibility of being a dog owner also includes being able to provide for their needs so before you take one home make sure that you can keep up with the expenses.

In this section you will receive an overview of the initial costs and monthly costs to keep a Saint Bernard as your pet.

Tip: Before buying anything, try to do a window shopping first, so you can compare prices as well as its quality.

Initial Costs

The initial costs for keeping a Saint Bernard include those costs that you must cover before you can bring your dog home. Some of the initial costs you will need to cover include your dog's crate, food/water bowls, toys and accessories, microchipping, spay/neuter surgery, initial vaccinations, and supplies for grooming and nail clipping – it also includes the cost of the dog itself.

Here are the estimated prices of each of these needs as well as an overview for the total price you need to pay in order to get and maintain a dog:

- **Cost of the Dog**

The cost to purchase a Saint Bernard can vary greatly depending where you find the dog. Since these dogs are huge and high maintenance, it can be very expensive; the average cost for a Saint Bernard is $1,800 or £1,419.70 and above. You can adopt a rescue Saint Bernard for as little as $800 or £630.98 but purchasing a puppy, especially a purebred puppy from an AKC-registered breeder, could be much more costly. Just be cautious when buying from unregistered breeders and do a background check on their credibility. Make sure the puppy is completely healthy.

- **Crate**

Since Saint Bernard dogs are huge breeds, you should consider buying a larger crate. Otherwise, you may need to constantly buy a bigger one especially when it reaches full adult size. The average cost for a big dog crate is about $50 and above in most cases.

- **Indoor Fences/Gates**

Indoor Fences or gates will serve as your dog's own space, aside from the crate; you'll need to create a boundary for your puppy that he can acknowledge as his own where you will set up his bed and toys. The average cost for these fences/gates is $100 or £70.

- **Bed**

You may want your Saint Bernard to be as comfortable as possible so a bed may come in handy. It is ideal to teach your puppy early on that there is a designated place for him to sleep. On average these bed cost about $40 or £38.

- **Food/Water Bowls**

Food and water bowls are just as important as providing your dog with a crate and bed to sleep in, you have to make sure he has a set of high-quality food and water bowls. The best materials for these are stainless steel because it is easy to clean and doesn't harbor bacteria. Choose bowls that are heavy so that the dog won't be able to push or tip it over and make a mess. The average cost for a quality set of stainless steel bowls is about $20 or £18.

- **Toys**

Yes even dogs needs toys! If you give your Saint Bernard plenty of toys to play with it will keep him mentally stimulated, and will also serve as its form of exercise. Another factor is that toys will help in preventing your dog from chewing or eating your things or home furniture. To start out, plan to buy an assortment of toys for your dog until you learn what kind he prefers. You may want to budget a cost of $50 or around £45 for toys just to be sure you have enough to last through the puppy phase.

- **Micro-chipping**

Micro-chipping your dog is not really required but it is preferred. A microchip is something that is implanted under your dog's skin and it carries a number that is linked to your contact information.

In the United States and Europe there are no federal or state requirements saying that you have to have your dog micro chipped, but it can benefit you and your dog in the long run.

Why do you need this? Well for one thing, your Saint Bernard could slip out of his harness on a walk or lose his ID tag. If someone finds him without identification, they can take him to a shelter to have his microchip scanned. Like a license, this can serve as a tracker for your dog as well. The procedure takes just a few minutes to perform and it only costs about $30 or £19.50 in most cases.

- **Initial Vaccinations**

Just like babies, puppies will require a number of different vaccinations. If you purchase your puppy from a reputable breeder, he might already have had a few but you'll still need more over the next few months as well as booster shots each year. You should budget about $50 or £32.50 for initial vaccinations just to be prepared.

- **Spay/Neuter Surgery**

If you don't want unwanted pregnancies or "illegitimate puppies" it is best to let your dog undergo spay (for females) or neuter (for males) surgery. Basically this is a procedure where dogs' reproductive capabilities are removed. If you don't plan to breed your dog you should have him or her neutered or spayed before 6 months of age. The cost for this surgery will vary depending where you go and on the sex of your dog. If you go to a traditional veterinary surgeon, the cost for spay/neuter surgery could be very high but you can save money by going to a veterinary clinic. The average cost for neuter surgery is $50 to $100 or £32.50 - £65 and spay surgery costs about $100 to $200 or £65 - £130.

- **Dog Accessories and Extra Supplies**

Just like humans, dogs also have extra accessories that can come in handy. In addition to purchasing your dog's crate and food/water bowls, you should also purchase some basic grooming supplies as well as a leash and harness. The cost for these items will vary depending on the quality, but you should budget about $100 or £32.50 for these extra costs.

Initial Costs for Saint Bernard		
Needs	**One Dog**	**Two Dogs**
Purchase Price	$800 to $1,800 (£630.98 - £1,419.70)	$1,600 - $3,600 (£1261.95 - £2839.40)
Crate	$50 (£39.44)	$100 (£78.87)
Fences/Gates	$100 (£78.87)	$100 (£78.87)
Bed	$40 (£31.55)	$80 (£63.10)
Food/Water Bowl	$20 (£15.77)	$40 (£31.55)
Toys	$50 (£39.44)	$100 (£78.87)
Microchipping	$30 (£23.66)	$60 (£47.32)
Vaccinations	$50 (£39.44)	$100 (£78.87)
Spay/Neuter	$50 to $200 (£39.44 - £157.74)	$100 to $400 (£78.87 - £315.49)
Dog Accessories & Extra Supplies	$100 (£78.87)	$100 (£78.87)
Total	$1,290 to $2,290 (£1017.45 - £1806.17)	$2, 380 to $4,380 (£1877.16 – £3454.60)

*Costs may vary depending on location
**U.K. prices based on an estimated exchange of $1 = £0.79

Monthly Costs

After getting the basic needs of your dog, now comes the monthly things you need to buy and add on your budget. The monthly costs for keeping a Saint Bernard as a pet include those costs which recur on a monthly basis such as food, and other extra costs. In addition to food, however, you'll also need to think about things like annual license renewal, toy replacements, and veterinary exams.

Here are the estimated prices of each of these needs as well as an overview for the total monthly price you need to pay in order to get and maintain a dog:

- **Food and Treats**

Your Saint Bernard needs a healthy diet in order to maintain its muscular body; feeding them the right food is very important for his health and wellness. A high-quality diet for dogs is quite expensive, so you should be prepared to spend around $60 or around £47.32 on a large bag of high-quality dog food which will last you at least a month. You should also include a monthly budget of about $10 or £7.89 for treats.

- **License Renewal**

The cost to license your Saint Bernard will generally be about $25 or £19.72 and you can renew the license for the same price each year. You need to set aside about $2 or £1.58 per month over the course of a year.

- **Veterinary Exams**

Saint Bernard like any other pets needs to be regularly checked up in order to prevent any diseases. After he passes puppyhood, you should take him to the veterinarian at least every six months. You might have to take him more often for the first 12 months to make sure he gets his vaccines on time. The average cost for a vet visit is about $40 or £31.55 so, if you have two visits per year, it averages to about $7 or £5.52 per month. However, depending on how healthy or unhealthy your dog is, this amount is relative to the medical care he will need.

- **Extra Costs**

Aside from providing your Saint Bernard's food, license renewal, and vet visits there are also some other cost you might have to pay occasionally. These costs might include things like replacements for worn-out toys, a larger harness as your puppy grows, grooming or cleaning products, and more. You should budget about $15 or £11.83 per month for these extra costs.

Monthly Costs for Saint Bernard		
Monthly Needs	**One Dog**	**Two Dogs**
Food and Treats	$70 (£55.21)	$140 (£110.42)
License Renewal	$2 (£1.58)	$4 (£3.60)
Veterinary Exams	$7 (£5.52)	$14 (£12.60)
Other Costs	$15 (£11.83)	$30 (£19.50)
Total	$94 (£74.14)	$188 (£148.28)

*Costs may vary depending on location
**U.K. prices based on an estimated exchange of $1 = £0.79

What are the Advantages and Disadvantages of Owning a Saint Bernard?

Owning a Saint Bernard has its own pros and cons, it's not a perfect dog but its unique characteristics can match yours which can make them a perfect companion for you. So if you're one of those people who has fallen for the charm of the Saint Bernard, it would be wise to get to know more about having them as a pet and the best way to help you decide is to learn their good side and the not so good side about them so that you'll know what you will be dealing with. In this section you will find a list of the advantages and disadvantages for the Saint Bernard breed.

Pros for the Saint Bernard Breed

- Naturally adorable and fun, you will never get bored when you have them around
- Great watch dogs because of their size and alertness
- Generally gentle and friendly with everyone they meet
- Affectionate and loving especially with their owners which makes them great companions
- Does not bark excessively
- Adaptable
- Suited for apartment living even if they're huge, because they're quite dogs
- Not fussy – calm and easygoing
- Can follow orders and easy to take anywhere and no need to worry too much about getting easily hurt; not wild
- Generally likes to keep themselves clean

Cons for the Saint Bernard Breed

- Not so easy to groom, they have a thick coat so you may need some time and money to maintain it
- May need regular exercise
- Prone to health issues
- Does not do well when left alone, needs constant attention, suffers from separation anxiety
- Has a tendency to become (too) clingy
- Not suited for warm and humid weather, needs air-conditioning; Saint Bernard thrived naturally in cold weathers
- Must tolerate wheezing, snorting, snoring, slobbering and gassiness
- Acquires doggy odor if not bathed regularly

In summary, more expensive and high maintenance than other breeds in several aspects

Chapter Three: Purchasing Saint Bernard

You have seen the good side and the bad sides of a Saint Bernard, you already have enough knowledge on what you will be dealing with and you already have an idea of how much keeping this adorable pet would cost you, yet you are still here? Congratulations! Saint Bernard is just what you need! You have approximately 8 to 10 years of fun and laughter, love and affection, with a sprinkling of grumbles and troublesomeness here and there. In this chapter, you will know where and who you should buy from as well as how and what you need to do in your home.

Where Can You Buy a Saint Bernard?

Now that you've decided that Saint Bernard is the breed you want to have as a pet companion, it's time to prove it! Searching for that dog that will capture your heart the moment you laid eyes on them can be tough both in the dog world and the real world – so to speak. So here are some suggestions and tips on where you can find your one true love!

AKC and the Kennel Club Registered Breeders

If you want a puppy or dog that is of high quality, look no further, just go over the American Kennel Club's website and search for breeders of Saint Bernard. You can even scout a few breeders who are located near your area before making your choice. AKC-registered breeder in the United States or a Kennel Club-registered breeder in the U.K are legitimate quality breeders that passed the standards of these clubs or organizations, thus you can be sure that your puppy comes from a reputable breeder.

If you visit the website for either of these organizations you can find a list of breeders for all of the club-recognized breeds. You can also look for breeders on the website for other breed clubs like the Saint Bernard Club of America or The Saint Bernard Club of England. Even if these organizations don't provide a list of breeders you may be able to speak with members to find out more.

Rescue Shelter

Another great source of finding puppies aside from checking registered breeders is from a local rescue shelter. You can adopt these dogs who have been rescued and you can be sure that they are raised and trained well.

There are many benefits associated with rescuing an adult dog. For one thing, adoption fees are generally under $200 which is much more affordable than the $800 to $1,800 fee to buy a puppy from a breeder. Plus, an adult dog will already be housetrained. As an added bonus, most shelters spay/neuter their dogs before adopting them out so you won't have to pay for the surgery yourself. Another benefit is that an adult dog has already surpassed the puppy stage so his personality is set – with a puppy you can never quite be sure how your puppy will turn out.

Puppy Mills and Pet Stores

Now here are examples of places where you shouldn't buy a puppy. It is highly recommended that you don't get one from a puppy mill and even a pet store, although you may still find your pet here and it's still up to you to make that decision. This is only for the purpose of getting informed and exercising precaution.

A puppy mill is a type of breeding facility that focuses on breeding and profit more than the health and wellbeing of the dogs. Puppy mills usually keep their dogs in squalid conditions, forcing them to bear litter after litter of puppies with little to no rest in between. Many of the breeders used in puppy mills are poorly bred themselves or unhealthy to begin with which just ensures that the puppies will have the same problems.

Usually puppies from puppy mills end up in pet stores and unfortunately they sell the puppies to unsuspecting and poor informed dog lovers. Indeed, the puppies at the pet store might look cute and cuddly, but the downside is that there is no way to know whether they are actually healthy or well-bred. Puppy mill puppies are often already sick by the time they make it to the pet store, often traveling across state lines to get there.

The only time you should bring home a puppy from a pet store is if the store has a partnership with a local shelter and that is where they get their dogs. If the pet store can't tell you which breeder the puppies came from, or if they don't offer you any paperwork or registration for the puppy, it is likely that the puppy came from a puppy mill.

In this section, you will be provided with a list of reputable breeders and legit rescue shelters across United States and UK:

United States Breeders and Rescues:

Saint Bernard Club of America
<http://saintbernardclub.org/looking-for-a-saint-bernard/breeder-listing/>

Johnson Farms
<http://www.johnsonfarms.org/>

Opdyke Kennel
<http://www.opdykekennel.com/>

Hallelujah Saint Bernards
<http://www.hallelujahstbernards.com/>

Woodcrest Saints
<http://www.woodcrestsaints.com/contact.php>

West Wind Saints
<http://www.westwindsaints.com/puppiesforsale.html>

Lasquite Saint Bernards

<http://www.lasquitesaintbernards.com/>

Epic Saint Bernards

<http://www.epicsaintbernards.com/available>

Nerthus Kennels

<http://nerthuskennels.net/>

Saint Rescue

<http://www.saintrescue.org/>

Colorado Saint Bernard Rescue

<http://coloradosaintbernardrescue.org/>

Saint Bernard Rescue

<http://saintbernardrescue.org/>

Gentle Giants Rescue

<http://www.gentlegiantsrescue.com/saint_bernards.htm>

Saints Among Us

<http://www.saintsamongus.org/>

Saintly Bernards Rescue

<http://saintlybernards.org/>

Saint Bernard Rescue of Tennessee

<http://saintbernardrescuetn.myresq.org/>

Adopt a Pet

<http://www.adoptapet.com/s/adopt-a-saint-bernard>

Pet Finder

<https://www.petfinder.com/dog-breeds/Saint-Bernard>

United Kingdom Breeders and Rescues:

Gwillhill Saint Bernards

<http://www.gwilihillsaints.co.uk/>

Eminence Saint Bernards

<http://www.eminencestbernards.com/for-sale>

Kennel Club Rescue

<http://www.thekennelclub.org.uk/services/information/find/St.+Bernard.rescue>

Eurobreeder

<http://www.eurobreeder.com/breeds/saint_bernhardshund.html>

St. Bernard Trust Rescue

<http://www.stbernardtrust.com/Pages/default.aspx>

DogsBlog Rescue

<http://www.dogsblog.com/category/st-bernard/>

Pets4Homes UK

<http://www.pets4homes.co.uk/adoption/dogs/saint-bernard/>

Rain Rescue UK

<http://www.rainrescue.co.uk/pet/claude-gorgeous-young-st-bernard/>

Saint Bernards Needing Homes

<http://www.preloved.co.uk/classifieds/pets/dogs/all/uk/st+bernard>

How to Choose a Reputable Saint Bernard Breeder

Once you are ready to scout a puppy around your place, the best place to start is from legitimate organizations. A simple internet search will probably give you a variety of results however; you need to make sure that these breeders are reputable so that you wouldn't waste your time with it. Try searching or contacting representatives from AKC in United States or The Kennel Club in England so that they can refer you to reputable breeders around your area. You can also ask from other legit organizations such as the Saint Bernard Club of America for recommendations.

Once you have an initial list of these breeders, you can now compile a list of breeders from whatever sources you can and then take the time to go through each option to determine whether the breeder is reputable and responsible or not. You do not want to run the risk of purchasing a puppy from a hobby breeder or from someone who doesn't follow responsible breeding practices. If you aren't careful about where you get your puppy, you could end up with a puppy that is already sick.

In this section, you will learn a step-by-step process on what to do when it comes to searching the right breeder for you.

Step 1: Search and Visit the Breeder's Website
Check the website for each breeder on your list and look for key points about the breeder's history and experience. Take note of the following:

- Check for club registrations and a license, if applicable.
- If the website doesn't provide any information about the facilities or the breeder you are best just moving on.

Step 2: Contact the Breeders
After weeding out some breeders' websites, it's now time to personally talk to them to see how passionate and involved they are with these dogs.

Ask the breeder the following questions:

- How old are the parents?
- Can you provide me with the health clearances of the parents?
- Why did you decide upon this particular breeding?
- Can you tell me about the dogs in the 3 generation pedigree?
- How did you raise the puppies? Have you started training and socializing?
- Can you provide references from previous buyers?

Tip: Here are the answers you need to expect from them to know if they are really knowledgeable about these dogs:

- The female dog must not be younger than 18 months and the male should not be younger than 12 months. Dogs must be given time to mature before being bred.
- The breeder must be able to present you with a Canine Health Information Center number as an assurance that the parents were screened and deemed healthy and fit to be bred.
- The answer should have been well-thought out and it should include a rational objective.
- A good breeder will be able to give you a detailed account of the 3 generation pedigree without batting an eyelash because he knows it by heart and he is proud of it.

- The breeder should have already started introducing the world to the puppy and should be able to teach you how to continue training and socialization.
- A good breeder stays in touch with the owners to provide assistance so he should be able to give you references.

Bonus Points: If the breeder asks you questions about yourself as well that's a great sign that he/she is a reputable breeder. If they really care about these pets, they also would want to make sure that these puppies are in good hands.

Schedule an Appointment

Now that you have talked to your candidates, it's time to see for yourself! Visit the facilities for the remaining breeders on your list after you've weeded a few more of them out.

- Ask for a tour of the facilities, including the place where the breeding stock is kept as well as the facilities housing the puppies.
- If things look unorganized or unclean, do not purchase from the breeder.
- Make sure the breeding stock is in good condition and that the puppies are all healthy-looking and active.

A Few More Things to Remember…

After narrowing down your list to a final few options, you may want to interact with the puppies to make your decision. You won't find your puppy; your puppy will find you!

- Make sure the breeder provides some kind of health guarantee and ask about any vaccinations the puppies may have already received.
- Put down a deposit, if needed, to reserve a puppy if they aren't ready to come home yet.

Tips for Selecting a Healthy Saint Bernard Puppy

When selecting a puppy, make sure that you do not let yourself become caught up in the excitement of all its cuteness. Sure puppies are adorable but not all of them match your personality, so take the time to make a careful selection. If you rush the process you could end up with a puppy that isn't healthy or one whose personality isn't compatible with you or your family.

Here are some tips that may come in handy when selecting a healthy puppy:

Tip #1: Ask the breeder to give you a tour of the facilities, especially where the puppies are kept.

- Make sure the facilities where the puppies are housed are clean and sanitary – if there is evidence of diarrhea; do not purchase one of the puppies because they may already be sick.
- Take a few minutes to observe the litter as a whole, watching how the puppies interact with each other. The puppies should be active and playful, interacting with each other in a healthy way. Avoid puppies that appear to be lethargic and those that have difficulty moving – they are most probably sick.

Tip #2: Check the puppies and see how they react to you.

- It's already a red flag if the puppies appear frightened when you approach them, because it only means that they may not be properly socialized and you do not want a puppy like that. Some of the puppies may be somewhat cautious, but most of them should be very friendly, curious and interested in you.
- Let the puppies approach you and give them time to sniff and explore you before you interact with them. Take the opportunity to see their personalities, pet the puppies and encourage them to play with a toy. Single out any of the puppies that you think might be a good fit and spend a little time with them.
- Pick up the puppy and hold him to see how he responds to human contact.

The puppy should be affectionate and playful. It shouldn't be frightened of you and it should enjoy being pet.

Tip #3: Check the body of the puppies and look for any signs of illnesses.

- The puppy should have clear, bright eyes with no discharge. The coat should be even, no patches of hair loss or discoloration.
- The ears should be bat ears, clean and clear with no discharge or inflammation.
- The nose should be black. The only time lighter colored noses are acceptable is if the dog's color is lighter as well.
- If you're entertaining the idea of entering your Saint Bernard in shows, don't purchase the following colors: solid black, black and tan, black and white. These are disqualifications for the breed standard.
- The puppy's stomach may be round but it shouldn't be distended or swollen.
- The puppy should be able to walk and run normally without any mobility problems.

Final Tip: Once you've decided the puppy you're going to get, look them in the eye and try to be one with them. Your instinct will tell you if you have chosen the right one.

A Few More Things to Remember...

Once you've chosen your puppy, ask the breeder about the next steps. Do not take the puppy home if it isn't at least 9 or 10 weeks old because Saint Bernard dogs may become petulant and nasty when separated from their mothers and their litter too soon. And of course you have to make sure that it has been fully weaned and is already eating solid food.

Puppy-Proofing Your Home

While you're still waiting for your puppy to arrive, usually it may take a few days or so depending on the breeder and paper work, you can prepare by puppy-proofing your home. Puppy proofing or dog proofing is the process of making your home safe for your puppy. It usually involves removing or storing away anything and everything that could harm your puppy. It might help for you to crawl around the house on your hands and knees, viewing things from your puppy's perspective to find potential threats. Put yourself in their position, this is sort of similar to baby proofing your house if you have kids

Here's what you need to do before your newfound puppy or dog arrives:

- Make sure your trash and recycling containers have a tight-fitting lid or store them in a cabinet.

- Put away all open food containers and keep them out of reach of your puppy.

- Store cleaning products and other hazardous chemicals in a locked cabinet or pantry where your puppy can't get them.

- Make sure electrical cords and blind pulls are wrapped up and placed out of your puppy's reach.

- Pick up any small objects or toys that could be a choking hazard if your puppy chews on them.

- Cover or drain any open bodies of water such as the toilet, and outdoor pond, etc.

- Store any medications and beauty products in the medicine cabinet out of your puppy's reach.

- Check your home for any plants that might be toxic to dogs and remove them or put them out of reach.

- Block off fire places, windows, and doors so your puppy can't get into trouble.

- Close off any stairwells and block the entry to rooms where you do not want your puppy to be.

Chapter Four: Caring and Maintenance for a Saint Bernard

Now that you have enough knowledge on the basics and practical aspects of keeping a Saint Bernard as a pet, the next thing you need to learn is how to take care of your dog and be familiar with the tasks involved in maintaining them. This section talks about his habitat and exercise requirements, and will teach you how to prepare your home and make it an ideal environment for your puppy. It is vital for both you and your puppy that he has a space to call his own so that you can feel safe knowing that you have a way to keep him confined in your absence without always keeping him in a crate.

Caring Tips for Your Saint Bernard

Before bringing home your dog, the last thing you should do is to ask yourself if you are going to be able to put in the time and effort in caring for them. Below are some caring guideline tips that you need to be reminded of before taking on this journey with your dog.

Caring Tip#1: Spend time with your dog

As mentioned earlier, these dogs don't like being alone or away from their owners for long periods of time because they can suffer from separation anxiety. Make sure that you spend enough time and attention with your dog. Otherwise it'll be cruel to subject them to that if you're just planning on leaving them at home all the time. If you can bring them to work that will be better, if not then make sure to spend adequate time with them when you come home

Caring Tip #2: Prepare for medical emergencies and expenses

Like humans, dogs have a tendency to get sick or undergo procedure one way or another, so in case of emergencies, just be sure that you have allotted a portion of your budget for these unexpected moments. Saint Bernard dogs can be high-maintenance in terms of medical conditions.

Caring Tip #3: Patience and Consistency is key

The great thing about owning these dogs is that, not only will you train them, but you will also learn something about yourself. When you are training a dog, it takes a lot of patience and consistent disciplinary actions for you to be able to raise a well-behaved breed. Ironically, these qualities are keys in improving yourself as well.

Caring Tip #4: Decide the House Rules

For owners with families, make sure that all your family members agree and acknowledge owning a dog. Once the decision is agreed upon, you can all discuss house rules and the distribution of tasks when caring for the dog (e.g. off-limits areas, feeding time, potty time, etc.)

Caring Tip #5: Assign roles or tasks for each family member

You can decide who is going to be in charge of cleaning, feeding, grooming and training the dog. However, it is also wise that you should assign only one member of the family who will be the primary authority figure of the dog and will be in charge of housebreaking and training at all times.

Habitat and Exercise Requirements of a Saint Bernard

Saint Bernard are nature-oriented dogs, these breed came from cold mountains and are naturally outdoors. The downside is that they may not be suited for small apartments, they can adapt easily but these dogs prefer lots of space to play and roam around with. The good news is that even if you live in an apartment, you won't have a problem with their barking and attitude. Saint Bernard dogs are quiet creatures and can be trained to behave.

It is highly recommended that you take them out for long walks or outdoor adventures on the weekend especially if you live in a small house. When walking your dog, be sure to lead the way to establish your authority. To prevent obesity, they may need a daily exercise for about 15 minutes or so. To prevent respiratory problems, do not exceed the physical activities allowed by their stamina and endurance. A sign that you should stop and let them rest is when they start panting. Furthermore, since these dogs have thick coats, they may not be suited to live in places that don't have air-conditioners to fight the heat of high-temperature days. Needless to say, they should be kept in cool places as much as possible. In case it is otherwise unavoidable, be sure to have cooling pads and drinking water for first aid if they got exhausted from exercising.

It is recommended that you don't take them out for exercise on warm or humid days and definitely do not leave them under the sun for a long time. When you plan to stay outside for a long time—under tolerable weather conditions for your pet—you may need to apply canine sunscreen on your dog to prevent them getting sunburned.

For owners that have a pool or who are fond of beach trips, it is of utmost importance to know that your dog is not suited to be in the water too long. Constant supervision is a must when around dangerous-level waters. If ever your dog loves to go to the beach just make sure you look out for them and get safety gears such as a life vest if necessary.

Now, let's move on to how you can ensure that your dog feels at-home and is comfortable. First, you will need to provide him with certain things. A crate is one of the most important things you will need when you bring your new puppy home. Not only will it be a place for your puppy to sleep, but it will also be a place where you can confine him during the times when you are away from home or when you cannot keep a close eye on him. Your puppy will also need some other basic things like a water bowl, a food bowl, a harness, a leash, toys, and grooming supplies.

When shopping for food and water bowls, safety and sanitation are the top two considerations. Stainless steel is the best material to go with because it is easy to clean and resistant to bacteria. Ceramic is another good option. Heavy bowls are also a plus because the puppy will be unable to tip it over or push it across the floor which will save you from cleaning unnecessary mess. Avoid plastic food and water bowls because they can become scratched and the scratches may harbor bacteria.

Also remember that it is important to opt for a harness instead of a collar for this breed, and you should choose one that is appropriate to his size. This may mean that you will purchase several harnesses and leashes while your puppy is still growing. A harness will be helpful during leash training because it will improve your control over your puppy.

Provide your puppy with an assortment of different toys and let him figure out which ones he likes. Having a variety of toys around the house is very important because you'll need to use them to redirect your puppy's natural chewing behavior as he learns what he is and is not allowed to chew on. As for grooming supplies, you'll need a rubber gloves or soft bristle brush for daily brushing.

Above all, what you need to remember is that the Saint Bernard will thrive in a home where he is showered with attention and love.

Preparing Your Puppies Crate

Before you bring your puppy home, you should set up a particular area in your home for him to call his own. The ideal setup will include your puppy's crate, a comfy dog bed, his food and water bowls, an assortment of toys, and litter trays since this breed are indoor dogs. You can arrange all of these items in a small room that is easy to block off using indoor fences or gates, or you can use a puppy playpen to give your puppy some free space while still keeping him somewhat confined. It would be ideal to choose a room where most of the activity in the house happens so that your puppy won't feel isolated.

When you bring your puppy home you'll have to work with him a lot to get him used to the crate. It is very important that you do this because the last thing you want is your puppy to form a negative association with the crate. If this happens, it will be very difficult to make your puppy forget it and it will most likely ruin your success at house training. It is vital that your puppy learns that the crate is his own special place, a place where he can go to relax and take a nap if he wants to. If you use the crate as punishment, your puppy will not want to use it.

To get your puppy used to the crate, try tossing a few treats into it and let him go fish them out. Feeding your puppy his meals in the crate with the door open will be helpful as well.

You can also incorporate the crate into your playtime, tossing toys into the crate or hiding treats under a blanket in the crate. As your puppy gets used to the crate you can start keeping him in it with the door closed for short periods of time, working your way up to longer periods. Just be sure to let your puppy outside before and after you confine him and never force him to stay in the crate for longer than he is physically capable of holding his bowels and his bladder.

Chapter Five: Feeding Your Saint Bernard

Saint Bernard dogs can be quite high maintenance as what this book has established so far, this means that their nutritional needs should be of high – quality too. If you feed your dog the right nutrition and proper food, you can expect them to be healthy and it will also be an investment for you in the long run. A good nutrition will lead to a good sick free life. You will save a lot of money on expensive medical bills if you will be willing to put the time to properly nourish them with the right food. In this chapter, you will be given basic guidelines on feeding your dog and specific high-quality brands that are the best recommendations for Saint Bernard.

The Nutritional Needs of Saint Bernard

Saint Bernard breed need high-quality dog food that is rich in protein, fats and carbohydrates from animal meat such as chicken and beef; they also need a fair amount of fiber and vitamins from various food sources.

Feeding your Saint Bernard is easy to prepare and find in your local supermarket. In this section you will find out why these nutrients are important and why you should look for it especially when you're choosing a dog food for your pet.

- **Protein**

  Protein is made up of amino acids and it is incredibly important for the growth and development of your St. Bernard's tissues, organs, and cells. Dogs require animal-based proteins like fresh meat and meat meals because it provides them with the essential amino acids they cannot produce on their own. Plant-based proteins are less biologically valuable for your dog, though they are not essentially harmful.

- **Carbohydrate**

Dogs do not have specific requirements for carbohydrate in their diet, but carbohydrates do provide dietary fiber as well as valuable vitamins and minerals. Your dog should get his carbohydrate from whole grains like brown rice or oatmeal – these are the most digestible sources. Gluten-free and grain-free alternatives like sweet potato and tapioca are also good choices. Just be sure to avoid low-quality carbohydrates made from corn and soy ingredients because they provide very little nutritional value – dog food companies just use them to add bulk to their products without increasing cost or nutritional value.

- **Fats**

Fat is the most highly concentrated source of energy available to your dog. Like protein, fats should come from animal-based sources like chicken fat and fish oil instead of plant-based sources like flaxseed or canola oil. You should make sure your Saint Bernard gets a balance of omega-3 and omega-6 fatty acids to ensure proper skin and coat health.

- **Vitamins and Minerals**

Your dog needs to get certain vitamins and minerals from his diet because his body cannot produce them on his own. The most important vitamins for dogs are vitamin D, vitamin A, vitamin C and vitamin E. Aside from vitamins; you may also want to include minerals in your dog's diet. Minerals are inorganic compounds, because of that your dog's body cannot synthesize them; it must come from his diet. The most important minerals for dogs include copper, calcium, phosphorus, potassium, sodium, and iron.

Selecting the Dog Food for Your Saint Bernard

When it comes to selecting food for your dog, it is important that you know how to read the food label and check the nutritional facts indicated, just so you can have an idea of what the food contains and so that you'll be able to easily compare it with other brands. In this section, you will know some tips on what to buy and how to know if it's the right food for your dog.

Choose the right commercial dog food

If you'll notice, it is very common among dog food brands that they have the same ingredients like chicken, meat, omega-fats etc. Quality dog food brands uses consistent source to ensure constant quality. There are 3 grades of dog foods these are store brand, premium brands and super premium brands. A lot of breeders recommend that you opt to buy a premium or super premium brand so that you can be sure of its nutritional quality. Store brands are very cheap and always available in supermarkets but it may not be a wise choice because of the ingredients inconsistency. You don't know if the ingredients of store brands came from imported sources that are not approved or you may not be sure if it passed the food and safety regulation or not. Most store brands contain artificial coloring and lots of unnecessary preservatives.

Ingredients lists for dog foods are assembled in descending order by volume – this means that the ingredients at the top of the list are present in the highest quantities. So, if a product lists something like deboned chicken or fresh turkey as the first ingredient, you can assume that the product is a good source of protein.

When perusing dog food labels, you are likely to come across meat meals like chicken meal or salmon meal. The word "meal" might turn you off, but it is actually a very good ingredient to have in a dog food. Fresh meats contain up to 80% water so, by the time the product is cooked, the actual volume of the meat is much lower than it was originally. Meat meals have already been cooked down to a moisture level around 10% so they are actually a much more concentrated source of protein than fresh meat.

In addition to high-quality proteins, you should also look for digestible carbohydrates like whole grains and fresh vegetables. Things like brown rice and oatmeal are valuable additions to a commercial dog food while products like corn gluten meal or wheat flour are not. Gluten-free and grain-free carbohydrates like sweet potato and tapioca starch are also good ingredients if you are looking for a product that is free from gluten and grains. Just try to avoid byproduct meals as well as corn and soy ingredients. When it comes to fats, you should look for animal-based fats like chicken fat and salmon oil – these are much more biologically valuable to your dog than plant-based fats like canola oil or flaxseed. You should look for a blend of both omega-3 and omega-6 fatty acids as well.

Feed Your Dog the Right Amount

When it comes to feeding your St. Bernard, you may be wondering how much food is too much. The St. Bernard is one of the many breeds prone to obesity and once your dog becomes obese it can be difficult for him to lose weight.

What you need to do is to follow the feeding recommendations on the dog food package or better yet, consult a veterinarian so that you'll know how much you need to feed your pet.

Foods Your Dog Needs to Avoid

When it comes to your dog's nutrition, just like any other pets, there are certain foods you need to avoid because it may harm them and cause illnesses. The list of toxic foods given below may not seem dangerous at all or you might think it's edible for humans but it may definitely affect your dog. You have been warned!

Here is the list of foods that can be toxic to dogs and should therefore be avoided:

- Alcohol
- Apple seeds
- Avocado
- Cherry pits
- Chocolate
- Coffee
- Garlic
- Grapes/raisins
- Hops
- Macadamia nuts
- Mold
- Mushrooms
- Mustard seeds
- Onions/leeks
- Peach pits
- Potato leaves/stems
- Rhubarb leaves
- Tea
- Tomato leaves/stems

- Walnuts
- Xylitol
- Yeast dough

If your dog accidentally eats any of these foods, contact the Pet Poison Control hotline right away at (888) 426 – 4435.

Chapter Six: Training Your Saint Bernard

Training dogs and raising children can always be likened to one another. Both are in need of a lot of patience and perseverance in order to properly execute the challenge it brings. Training dogs may cause you a lot of hard work and may tend to be exasperating in the first few days of training them, but the price of a well-trained dog is worth it. It has been established that Saint Bernard dogs are calm, friendly and obedient. Because of such traits, it makes it easier for them to learn and be trained. Since they can easily be trained, as pet owners, you must be attentive to both their needs and misbehaving because it leads you to a more effective training. In this chapter, you will be taught on how to introduce your puppy to their new home, and how will they be able to cope with socialization.

This chapter will also give you tips and tricks in effectively training and teaching your puppies.

Socializing Your New Saint Bernard Puppy

- Acquaint your puppy to his new friends in your home by introducing them.

- Call on your friends who have dogs and invite them to come and meet your new puppy your new puppy. It is always advisable that everyone is vaccinated accordingly.

- Expose your puppy to people of different gender with various sizes, shapes and skin color.

- Introduce your puppy to children of different ages. It is important that these children know how to handle puppies for their own safety.

- Walk your puppy in different places as much as you can so that he can expose with various surfaces and surroundings.

- Expose your puppy with water from hoses, sprinklers and showers, etc. Make sure that you have control over your puppy once they are introduces with bodies of water because leaving them unattended might drown them.

- Expose your puppy to water from hoses, sprinklers, showers, etc. Be sure to have control over your puppy when introducing him to bodies of water that could drown him.

- Do not forbid your puppy from hearing loud noises, such as fireworks, cars backfiring, loud music, thunder, etc. This will allow them to be less fearful in response to loud noises.

- Introduce your puppy to various appliances and tools such as blenders, lawn mowers, vacuums, etc.

- Walk your puppy with different types of harnesses and leashes.

- It is important for your puppy to be taken out to the dog park to interact with other dogs when he is already old enough to do so.

Positive Reinforcement for Obedience Training

Just like raising up children, reward system is a very effective way in training them to be more obedient. Dogs are not as challenging to train as we think, like children, reward system can also be applicable and effective to them. Once you reward your dog for their good behavior, there is a greater chance that they will repeat that behavior next time. This is what you call positive reinforcement training, which is the simplest and most effective method of training that you as a dog owner can use. Remember that positive reinforcement can also in the form of praising the good behavior of your puppy.

First, successful dog training is always a two-way process. It is important that as dog owners to make sure that your dog understands what you want from them. It will be very hard for them to follow what you have been asking them to do if they do not completely understand what you are asking them to do. They will tend to be unresponsive and they will also respond incorrectly to your command. You must guide your dog in what you are commanding them to perform what you are asking from them. By guiding them, you are able to lead them to the proper behavior that you are expecting them to perform. Once they finally perform the desired behavior, immediately praise them and reward them with a treat. This can help them associate the reward to the behavior that was being asked of them.

Secondly, consistency is very important in achieving successful dog training. Because your puppy is already learning how to obey to your commands, you must be consistent in rewarding him overtime he does what you asked of him. Consistency allows your puppy to better associate the reward to your desired behavior, therefore, they will repeat in obeying the command that you have rewarded them with. Training sessions should be kept short — around 5 to 10 minutes — to prevent your puppy from being disinterested and bored. Spread out your training sessions throughout the day, being frequent but short.

Negative Consequences for Respect Training

In training your dog, positive reinforcement is not enough. Remember that the good behavior of dogs should be praised and their bad behaviors must be disciplined. Dogs should also be trained to respect you as a dog owner by responding to you when you ask him to stop doing unwanted actions. This does not come off that easily, you must earn the respect of your dog. Saint Bernard dogs, especially males, may tend to be dominant and willful. It is important to establish your authority over them by enforcing respect training. In respect training, there are specific rules that must be established over them. The words "no" and "stop" have to be said to them whenever they misbehave. Avoid scolding or yelling at them that might cause them to sulk because they have very sensitive feelings. It is better to gently but firmly reprimand them for them to know that you are in authority over them, but at the same time, they will not be too fearful of your presence. Remember that consistency is very important. Be more consistent in your training. Consistency leads to success.

Crate Training - Housebreaking Your Puppy

Obedience training is also another important thing your Saint Bernard should have. This is very important for your puppies because this establishes a good behavior as he grows up as an adult dog. Obedience training should be established and taught as young as possible because you cannot always be around following him with a pooper scooper. This is why housebreaking is very crucial when you get your new puppy. By using your crate appropriately, you will be able to help to establish the rightful places for your puppy's needs. When you are at home and able to watch over your pet dog, always lead them to the area where their litter tray is located and keep him in that same room to give him a chance to do what he has to do. Make commands like, "Go pee" and lead them to the litter tray so that he will be guided on the right area where he has to do a certain thing. Always remember to reward him every time he is successful with his task.

Of course, you will not be able to watch your puppy overnight so it is advisable to keep them inside their crate. Their crate should be spacious enough for them to be able to move around, stand up, turn around, and lie down. When you give him enough space for all these activities to be done, he will see his crate as a den that he will be comfortable staying in. Also, remember not to let your puppy stay in the crate for a time that he might not be able to hold his bladder. Take him out to pee before he is placed in the crate and immediately after he comes out.

Housetraining will eventually be effective if your puppy gets enough opportunity to do his business in his litter tray, gets rewarded consistently, and when he gets comfortable in his crate without the need of you watching over him. The effect and the length of training will still be dependent on your St. Bernard's ability to respond and obey. With so much reiteration, consistency, patience, and positive reinforcement are the key to successful litter training.

Teaching Tricks and Playing Games

A fun way of training your Saint Bernard dog is to incorporate teaching tricks with play time. This will not only help you teach them tricks, but this also a way that you can spend quality time with them. This will also allow your puppy to associate tricks to fun and enjoyment, rather than a boring task that must be learned. This can also help your dog to have the exercise that his body needs. Positive reinforcement is very important in teaching tricks. Once a treat or a praise is given, they are likely to repeat what was commanded of them because it will always be associated with a positive remark. Avoid punishing your dog when they are not able to perform the trick that you asked them to do.

Play Fetch – This is one of the most useful tricks that your dog needs to learn. This can be a great form of exercise for your dog as he moves around. This is also an avenue when you can teach him new words and commands. This is a very effective way of teaching your puppy because it incorporates play, exercise and training. An easy way to help him get started with fetching is to start with items that will excite him like a ball, a chew toy or a bone. It is important to label the item that you are asking him to retrieve repeatedly before throwing it and once he returns it. Do not forget to give him a reward when he does a great gob. When you have properly labeled the items that you are using, this can develop his vocabulary. With that, you do a game that enables him to identify a specific item among a lot more items surrounding it. It is good to also increase the reward to motivate him better.

Play Hide and Seek – By using the words that he has learned from playing fetch, you can incorporate the game of hide and seek with it. You can make use of the objects he already knows but instead of asking him to fetch it, teach him how to hide it and how to look for it. Saint Bernard will love this game because they are fond of hiding things and looking for them later on. Reward him respectively for every object that has been retrieved.

Commands – This trick can be used to establish discipline. Aside from playing fetch this could be used for him to know how to his litter trays to relieve his bladder or bowels, and to the other places where he needs to go to. Just like the command fetch, you have to first lead and point him to the place. Then, you have to make sure that you repeatedly and properly identify it. Don't forget to give a reward when he gets it right.

Chapter Seven: Grooming Your Saint Bernard Properly

As you may have noticed and read from the history section of this book, the St. Bernard breed were born and raised in winter. It is natural for them to have a long and thick coat to protect them from the cold winds of the Swiss Alps Mountains. Thick and long fur means only thing – high maintenance grooming, because of their long coats, grooming tasks can mean a lot of work and time-consuming compared to dogs with short hair or fur. Don't worry this is the purpose of this chapter. It will teach you tips and tricks on how to groom your Saint Bernard properly.

Recommended Tools for Grooming Your Dog

Before getting to the process of grooming your dog, you need to buy materials for your dog. These will help you in carrying out the grooming task properly and with ease. Here's the list of several recommended grooming tools and supplies you need:

- Rubber gloves or soft bristle brush
- Nail clippers
- Dog-friendly ear cleaning solution
- Organic Oatmeal dog shampoo (oatmeal is optional)
- Dry cloth
- Dog toothbrush
- Dog-friendly toothpaste
- Any Moisturizer or lotion for dogs
- Petroleum jelly
- Baby powder
- small toothbrush

Grooming Process of Saint Bernard Dogs

Now that you know what tools and supplies you need to have on hand for grooming your Saint Bernard you are ready to learn the process. Since your St. Bernard's coat is thick and long, it is highly recommended that you brush their coat as often as possible – at least once a day is needed to keep your dog's skin and coat soft and silky.

Here are some tips on how to comb and also bathe your St. Bernard's coat:

Tip #1: Start from the head

The first thing you need to do is to start brushing the back of your dog's head and work your way down the dog's neck and back, brushing in the direction of hair growth. Move on to the dog's sides and comb the fur down each leg. Once you've gone over your Saint Bernard with a comb to remove tangles you can do it again with the wire pin brush to collect loose and dead hairs. For dogs that are particularly high shedder (your dog could be one of them) try using an undercoat rake to remove dead hairs from the Saint Bernard's undercoat before they can be shed.

Tip #2: Bathe your dog in moderation

Unlike humans, dogs don't need to take bath often, not because they are not hygienic but because it could be dangerous for their health. Frequent bathing is not necessary, try to just keep it in moderation; at least once or twice a week is fine. You should only do it when he really needs it. If you bathe your dog too frequently it could cause his skin and coat to dry out. When you do bathe your dog, be sure to use dog-friendly shampoo that will be gentle on his skin.

Here are some guidelines for bathing your Saint Bernard:

- Place a non-slip mat or towel on the bottom of your tub then fill it with a few inches of warm water (not hot water).

- Put your Saint Bernard in the tub and use a handheld sprayer or a container to wet down his coat as thoroughly as possible.

- Apply a small amount of your dog-friendly shampoo to your hand then work it into your Saint Bernard's coat, forming a thick soapy lather.

- Work the soap through the hair on your dog's neck, back, legs, chest and tail – avoid getting his ears, eyes, and nose wet.

- Thoroughly rinse away the soap using clean water until all traces have been removed.

- Use a damp wash cloth to carefully clean the fur on your dog's head and face, if necessary, keeping the eyes and ears dry.

- Towel-dry your Saint Bernard using a large fluffy towel until you have already removed as much moisture from his coat as possible.

- You must keep your dog's ears dry. Wet ears are a breeding ground for bacteria and infection. The Saint Bernard doesn't have an erect and floppy ears that will allow plenty of airflow to the ear canal that is why there is a huge risk for ear infections so be very careful.

Other Grooming Tasks Your Dog Needs

Grooming doesn't stop in just brushing or maintaining your dog's hair, there are also some other grooming tasks involved such as trimming your dog's nails, cleaning his ears, and brushing his teeth.

- **How to Brush Your Saint Bernard's Teeth**

The idea of brushing your dog's teeth might sound gross but it is actually a very important part of grooming. Periodontal (dental) disease is incredibly common among pets and it can actually lead to some serious health problems including tooth loss, heart disease, and organ damage.

Here are some simple tips on how to brush your dog's teeth and mouth:

- Place a small amount of dog-friendly toothpaste on a dog toothbrush.
- Brush just a few of your dog's teeth at a time until he gets used to the process.
- Be sure to reward your dog after brushing his teeth so he learns that good behavior earns him a treat. This will make things much easier for you in the long run.

- **How to Clean Your Saint Bernard's Ears**

Cleaning your Saint Bernard's ears isn't a difficult task, but he might not like it. A dog's ears are a breeding ground for bacteria so, if you do not keep them clean, your dog may have an increased risk for recurrent ear infections.

Here are some simple tips on how to brush your dog's teeth and mouth:

- Clean your dog's ears, add a few drops of a dog-safe ear cleaning solution to your dog's ear canal.
- Massage the outside of your Saint Bernard's ears by hand to spread the solution.
- Use clean cotton balls to clean away any buildup inside your dog's ears (as well as excess cleaning solution).
- Let your dog's ears dry.

- **Nail Clipping for Your Dog**

Each of your dog's nails contains a quick – the blood vessel that supplies blood to the nail. That is why when it comes to trimming your dog's nails, you need to be very careful. If you cut the nail too short and sever this blood vessel it could not only hurt your dog, but it could cause profuse bleeding as well. The best way to prevent this from happening is to make sure you have the right tool and to learn the proper nail trimming procedure before you do it yourself. Ask your vet or a professional groomer to show you how to trim your dog's nails and then, when you do it yourself, be sure to only trim away the sharp tip.

Chapter Eight: Breeding a Saint Bernard

It is important to understand that breeding should only be done by professional breeders who only aim to preserve and help the breed live longer by eliminating the genetic defects that cause oppressive health problems in the dogs. With this in mind and recalling that Saint Bernard has disastrous genes, breeding them is flat-out and forcibly discouraged. Your love for your dog should encompass the entire breed as well and you should only have their best interests at heart. Irresponsible breeding will most likely just cause damage to the female dog, the offspring and consequently to the entire breed. To further understand the controversy of breeding Saint Bernard, continue reading this chapter.

Basic Dog Breeding Information

Before 6 months of age, ASPCA recommends having your dogs neutered or spayed. The 6th month is the time the female dog experiences her first heat. Heat is the more simplified term for the estrus cycle in dogs. This cycle generally lasts for about 14 to 21 days. Generally, females are on heat twice a year, but it still varies from one dog to another. When your female dog goes into heat, this is when she is capable of becoming pregnant. Large dogs like Saint Bernard breed tend to be on heat for the first time at the age of two years old. This is true especially for giant and large dog breeds.

It is important that you wait until the female reaches sexual maturity until you start breeding them. Most breeders recommend waiting until the age of 2 years old to start breeding, though some dogs can reach their full size when they reach one year of age. This ensure that the dog is mature enough to physically carry and bear puppies, but it also provides enough time for any serious health problems to be spotted. Once you see your dog having signs of congenital health problems, it is more preferable to not breed her for a year or so. Dogs should only be bred preferably, every other year. Consecutive conception and giving birth within a short span of time causes problems in her reproductive system.

The details of heat and breeding come only after choosing the ideal breeding pair. Once female dog goes into heat there are visible signs that you can observe. First, check if the vulva is swelling and having a bloody discharge. This is a sign that the dog is on heat. Over the course of the heat cycle the discharge lightens in color and becomes more watery. In the 10th day of the cycle the discharge turns to light pink. This is a sign that she is beginning to ovulate, and also this is the time when she is most fertile. At this phase, this is the perfect time to introduce her to male dogs that you have chosen as ideal breeding partners. This may take time because she may not be able to respond right away. Be patient, this may take a while. You can try after a day or two once the female isn't responsive at first.

When a female dog is on heat, you do not have plans on breeding your female dog, keep her looked in. Male dogs can distinctly smell female dogs on heat even if they are miles away from each other. Make sure not to take a female dog out when she is on heat. The male sperm of a dog can survive for almost 5 days in the reproductive tract of the female dog. That is why it is important to keep female dogs away from stray dogs. Make sure to not leave her unattended.

If you have a desire to breed your dog, you must take note of the estrus cycle so that you know the perfect time to breed her. It may take a few years for the cycle to become regular, so you must be patient in keeping track when your female dog is on heat. Make sure to mark your calendar so you can be on track and updated once a pattern has been made so that the timing is perfect once you introduce her to the ideal breeding partner. Do not forget to give your dog a rest from breeding. One year is an ideal time to rest as to prevent problems in reproduction and birthing.

Breeding Tips and Raising Puppies

After the male dog fertilizes the egg inside the female's body, the gestation period will start in the female dogs. During that cycle, the puppies start to develop inside her womb of the female dog. The gestation period for Saint Bernard lasts for anywhere from 60 to 63 days with the average being 61. For a large breed like your Saint Bernard, it can extend for 5 more days. However, you won't be able to actually tell that your dog is pregnant until after the third week. By the 25th day of pregnancy it is safe for a vet to perform an ultrasound and by day 28 he should be able to feel the puppies by palpating the female's abdomen. At the six week mark an x-ray can be performed to check the size of the litter. Saint Bernard's average litter size is between 6-8 puppies per gestation. Some can reach until 10 puppies per litter, but survival rates can vary.

It is important to take good care of your pregnant Saint Bernard's. Feeding them with more food than the usual can come in the fourth of fifth week of pregnancy. This is usually the time when they start gain weight in the course of the pregnancy. Starting on the fifth week, you can already raise the daily increments of your dog's diet in proportion to her weight gain. A healthy and balanced diet is necessary for you pregnant dogs. Also, regular vet appointments should be followed to have a regular check-up of your Saint Bernard's progression in her pregnancy.

In about eight weeks of gestation, you female Saint Bernard dog must be ready to give birth. This process for the dogs is called whelping. In this time, you must be all packed and ready to transport your dog whenever she is ready to be taken to the vet to help her give birth under time pressure.

While your dog is getting ready to give birth, their internal temperature slight decreases. A good way of predicting when the puppies of your dog will be born is by checking her temperature once a day during the gestation week. As soon as your dog's body temperature drops to 100°F to 102°F (37.7°C to 38.8°C to about 98°F (36.6°C), labor is most likely to begin soon. This is a good method to predict when you are going to take your dog to the vet in the perfect time. There will be obvious signs of discomfort that will be seen in your dog as she reaches this state. Signs such as, pacing, panting and changing of positions will most likely be seen in her behavior. Make sure to keep an eye on her at this stage, but at the same time letting her do her own thing. You must be careful to watch over her to prevent her from having any complications in her giving birth.

In the early stage of labor, your dog will experience contractions. At this time, there will be a 10 minute difference in the contractions that she will be experiencing. Once your dog experiences contractions for 2 hours straight without giving birth, take her to the vet immediately. C-Section whelping and normal delivery is entirely different. One can never really tell which your dog will undergo through because it varies.

After whelping, it is necessary for the newborn puppies to start nursing right away. Just like newborn humans, they need to be able to ingest colostrum. Colostrum is the milk of the mother dog which contains a lot of essential vitamins and antibodies. It helps the newborn puppies be protected from any sickness while their immune system continues to develop. The mother dog will naturally encourage her puppies, it is important that she gets proper nutrition in her meal intake.

The newborn Saint Bernard puppies only weighs 1 ½ - 2 ½ pounds and they will continue growing over the next several months until they zone in on their adult size. It is very ideal to weigh your puppies once every week to keep track of their growth. It is important to keep the puppies close to their mother dogs to help them be warm because they are born with fine hair. Place your puppies on a well-lit place that is warm and cozy. Puppies are born with their eyes and ears closed eventually they will start to open from 10 to 12 days after birth.

The first few weeks of the puppy's life, they will be heavily dependent on the mother dog until they start to become more active. You can start offering your puppies with solid food soaked in broth and water in small amounts which starts the weaning process. After a few weeks the puppies will start to nurse less and eat more solid food. A Saint puppy will be completely weaned at 8 weeks of age. At this age, they are more active and can be separated with their mothers.

Chapter Nine: Showing Your Saint Bernard

Participating in dog shows are one of the joys of owning a pure-breed dog. If you are suggesting having this in mind, you should think about your dog if it has the confidence, a well-mannered stature, and if your dog is prepared for it. You also need to question your dedication, if you have the time and patience to do enter this task. If you are ready to do both of the tasks at hand and pursue this avocation then you must know if your Saint Bernard passed all the requirements of AKC to become a show dog. In this chapter, a summary of the standards of the AKC for a Saint Bernard would be discussed and also how you could prepare your dog for an amazing show.

Saint Bernard Breed Standard

Guidelines for both breeding and showing Saint Bernard's are provided in the AKC breed standard. All Saint Bernard owners who want to pursue in showing their dogs at AKC shows must compare with the official breed standard which AKC-registered breeders also follow these sets of standards in selecting dogs. These are the breeding standards for the American Saint Bernard breed:

General Appearance and Temperament

The Saint Bernard is a tall figure, which is strong and muscular in every part. He has a powerful and intelligent head. He is known to be friendly and sociable to the people he is around with.

Head and Neck

The skull of a Saint Bernard is massive and wide, a bit arched and its sides are sloped with a gentle curve into a very high and developed cheek bones. Its muzzle is short, does not taper. The vertical depth at the root should be greater than the length of the muzzle. The nose is very substantial, with broad nostrils and it is always black like the lips. Neck appears to be high and strong for this kind of breed.

Body and Tail

The chest should be well arched, averagely deep but not overreaching the elbows. Back should be large and perfectly straight. The belly should be set-off from the very strong loin section, only a bit drawn up. The tail should be starting with a wide and strong to a long rump and powerful tip.

Legs and Feet

The legs should be strong and straight but hocks should have moderate angulation (when it comes to the hind legs). Feet should be wide and with powerful toes a bit closed and with high knuckles.

Coat and Texture

The coat should be very dense and yet should be short haired, lying smoothly and a tough without any feeling of roughness.

Color

White and red should be present taking into the account the different shades of red. Brindle patches with white markings. Necessary markings are: white chest, feet and tip of tail, noseband collar or spot of the nape.

Size

Size should be 27 ½ inches for a male Saint Bernard, a female should be 25 ½ inches; female built is finer and more delicate.

Gait

Gait should be firm but free and energetic..

Disqualifications

- Swayback and a disproportionately long back
- Hock is too much bent
- Straight Hindquarters
- Upward growing hair in spaces between the toes
- Cow hocks
- Weak pasterns

Preparing Your Saint Bernard for Show

If you will be in an environment that has a lot of dogs and people, make sure that your Saint Bernard can socialize well.

- Your dog should able to hold his bladder for hours within a show so ensure y our dog is completely house trained
- He should learn how to listen and follow basic commands, solidify your dog's grasp of basic obedience
- Before you choose a show, you should do some research for specific for that show and check their

requirements, so you could know if your dog meets all the requirements for registration

- Have your vet clear his overall health for the show, make sure your dog has all the vaccinations that he needs (especially Bordetella because he will be around some dogs)
- Take the necessary steps to keep your dog's coat clean and in good condition, about a week before the show.
- Teach your Saint Bernard to slightly trot – not walk or run, let him stand squarely with his head held high also.

It is better for you to pack a bag of supplies that you will need on the day of the show, as you have already taken into account the requirements for the show and the AKC breed standard guidelines. This is a list for helpful things to put in your supply pack for your dog show:

- Information for registration
- Exercise pen or a dog crate
- Grooming tools
- Treats and food
- Water and food bowls
- Trash bags for poop
- Medications (if the veterinarian prescribes it)
- Clothes for changing
- Food and water that you need
- Rags or paper towels

- Toys for the dog

If you want to show your dog but you don't want to jump immediately into an AKC show, you may be able to find some local dog shows in your area. Local shows may be put on by a branch of a national Saint Bernard breed club and they can be a great place to learn and to connect with other owners.

Chapter Ten: Keeping Your Dog Healthy

Most minimal discomfort and the longest life possible is all we want for our dogs. In that retrospect, we should not take for granted nor neglect health care, especially for our dearly Saint Bernard breed. Unfortunately, this breed is more exposed in getting sick than most other breeds; it is a challenge for us to keep him healthy. As we have tackled in Chapter 2, in terms of medical costs they are amongst the most expensive. High-maintenance health care is what they need so before making a decision of getting one you need to make sure that you are ready to tackle the potential stress — with the worst situation possible — crippling heartbreak that these diseases could create. In this chapter, know the best ways of ensuring a long and healthy life for your dog, do him a favor and ensure it for him.

Common Health Problems Affecting Saint Bernard

Their health is the most problematic flaw of a Saint Bernard. Witnessing your dog suffers from illness and conditions which could lead to death is harder to deal than the stubbornness and difficulty of training them.

Prevention is better than cure, take the time to learn about the common struggles of health of the breed while it is early, so that you could be prepared and you are well equipped with knowledge when some of those events occur. In lieu of that, we will orient you about the common health risks that your Saint Bernard could have.

Some of the common conditions affecting Saint Bernard include Hip dyplasia, heat stroke, allergies, Intervertebral Disc Disease, vWD Disease and Degenerative Myelopathy

Hip Dysplasia

Hip dysplasia is a very common musculoskeletal problem among dogs especially for large breeds like St. Bernard. In a normal hip, the head of the femur (thigh bone) sits snugly within the groove of the hip joint and it rotates freely within the grove as the dog moves. Hip dysplasia occurs when the femoral head becomes separated from the hip joint – this is called subluxation. This could occur as a result of abnormal joint structure or laxity in the muscles and ligaments supporting the joint.

This condition can present in puppies as young as 5 months of age or in older dogs. Genetics are the largest risk factor for hip dysplasia, though nutrition and exercise are factors as well. Diagnosis for hip dysplasia is made through a combination of clinical signs, physical exam, and x-rays.

The most common symptoms of hip dysplasia include pain or discomfort, limping, hopping, or unwillingness to move. As the condition progresses, the dog's pain will increase and he may develop osteoarthritis. The dog may begin to lose muscle tone and might even become completely lame in the affected joint.

Surgical treatments for hip dysplasia are very common and generally highly effective. Medical treatments may also be helpful to reduce osteoarthritis and to manage pain.

Heat Stroke

Saint Bernard dogs are not built to endure heat, warm and humid weather. As established earlier, they have thick coats and they originally came from snowy mountains Because of this, they may have difficulty regulating their body temperature which could lead to a fatal heat stroke. It is important to keep your dog in cool temperatures and to make sure that he has access to water at all times.

Allergies

An allergy develops when the dog's immune system identifies a substance as pathogenic, or dangerous, and it launches an attack. Just like humans, dogs can develop allergic reactions to a number of different things. The three main types of allergens can be inhaled, ingested, or taken into the body through skin contact.

Surprisingly, food allergies tend to produce skin-related symptoms like itching and scratching rather than digestive symptoms. Chronic ear infections are also a common sign of food allergies in dogs. Common symptoms of allergies in dogs include red or itchy skin, runny eyes, increased scratching, ear infections, sneezing, vomiting, diarrhea, and swollen paws. Some common allergens for dogs include smoke, pollen, mold, dust, dander, feathers, fleas, medications, cleaning products, certain fabrics, and certain foods. For some environmental allergens, your vet might prescribe antihistamines or your vet might give your dog an injection to protect him. The best treatment for allergies is avoiding contact with the allergen.

Intervertebral Disc Disease (IDD)

IDD is the occurrence of a rupturing or herniating disc in the spine which then thrusts into the spinal cord. This disease is very painful and may render your dog weak and unwilling to move. This thrusting movement disables the nerve transmissions to mobilize along the spinal cord which may cause paralysis.

The symptoms of IVDD are highly variable and may include neck pain or stiffness, back pain or stiffness, abdominal tenderness, arched back, lameness, sensitivity to touch, stilted gait, reluctance to rise, loss of coordination, tremors, collapse, and paralysis. These symptoms most commonly present after strenuous activity of physical trauma. Intervertebral Disc Disease can be caused by trauma, age, or simply from a sudden jolt like a bad fall or a miscalculated jump. Surgery for extreme cases can only be administered within the first day of the injury. Medical treatments may involve corticosteroids or non-steroidal anti-inflammatories aimed to treat pain and control inflammation. Surgical treatments may help to decompress the spinal cord or to inject enzymes to help stabilize the affected disks.

Von Willebrand's Disease

This is a blood disorder that afflicts a lot of dog breeds, mainly involving the dysfunction of blood clotting. This disease is an inherited condition caused by genetic mutations that affect the synthesis, release and stability of vWF. In order to diagnose vWD, your veterinarian will perform a physical exam as well as a medical history. Blood count and blood chemical profiles will also be obtained along with a urinalysis and electrolyte panel.

A dog suffering from this disease will exhibit signs of excessive and abnormal bleeding. Lack of vWF can lead to excessive bleeding following even a minor injury. It may also cause nosebleeds, bloody urine, bloody stool, bleeding gums, and vaginal bleeding (in females). It can also cause bruising and anemia.

The good news is that there are existing treatments to help your dog cope with the illness such as searing and stitching wounds and blood transfusions before undergoing surgical procedures.

A transfusion with fresh plasma and fresh blood to increase the supply of vWF in the blood is the best treatment for this disease. Fortunately, this condition can be managed in mild to moderate cases. Dogs with more severe vWD may require additional transfusions for surgery and supportive care may be required following spontaneous bleeding episodes.

Degenerative Myelopathy

Degenerative myelopathy is a progressive disease which affects the spinal cord in older dogs. This disease typically manifests between 8 and 14 years of age, beginning with loss of coordination in the dog's hind limbs.

This disease is caused by degeneration of the white matter in the dog's spinal cord. This degeneration may or may not be caused by the mutation of a certain gene. In order to diagnose your Saint Bernard with degenerative myelopathy your veterinarian will perform tests to rule out other causes of the weakness. These tests may include MRI, myelography, and biopsy of the spinach cord. In many cases, however, the diagnosis cannot be completely confirmed except with an autopsy (necropsy).

At first the dog will wobble when walking or drag the feet – this might occur in one limb or both. As the disease progresses, the limbs become increasingly weak and the dog might have difficulty standing. Eventually, the weakness will worsen to the point of paralysis and the dog will be unable to walk.

Unfortunately, there are no treatments available to slow or stop the progression of degenerative myelopathy. The best treatment is to manage the dog's symptoms and to keep him as comfortable as possible. The use of harnesses and carts is common for dogs that have lost the use of their hind limbs.

Preventing Illness with Vaccinations

Providing a nutritious and balanced diet for your Saint Bernard could keep him healthy in the best way. Also, routine vaccinations and proper veterinary care should be ensured for your dog. Vaccinations could help guard him from specific communicable diseases like distemper, parvovirus, and rabies but it does not protect your dog from nutritional deficiencies or inherited conditions.

Certain regions have a higher risk for certain diseases, so the vaccinations of your Saint Bernard would vary. This vaccination schedule will help you keep track with when your dog needs to visit the vet, for the vet could give your dog's needs and vaccinations on when he needs them.

Consult this vaccination schedule, so that you have an idea what kind of vaccinations that your puppy needs:

Vaccination Schedule for Dogs**			
Vaccine	**Doses**	**Age**	**Booster**
Rabies	1	12 weeks	annual
Distemper	3	6-16 weeks	3 years
Parvovirus	3	6-16 weeks	3 years
Adenovirus	3	6-16 weeks	3 years
Parainfluenza	3	6 weeks, 12-14 weeks	3 years
Bordetella	1	6 weeks	Annual
Lyme Disease	2	9, 13-14 weeks	Annual
Leptospirosis	2	12 and 16 weeks	Annual
Canine Influenza	2	6-8, 8-12 weeks	Annual

** Keep in mind that vaccine requirements may vary from one region to another. Only your vet will be able to tell you which vaccines are most important for the region where you live.

Saint Bernard Care Sheet

Instructions and advices are given to you in this book by giving you a combination of valuable facts which could help you comprehensively understand how to take care a Saint Bernard as a pet. You will still find this book useful even when you have already decided to adopt your own Saint Bernard. Use this care sheet as a quick reference for basic information that you would like to recall, so you would not waste your time flipping through the entire book. This care sheet is a summary of all the useful information that an owner of a Saint Bernard needs.

Basic Saint Bernard Information

Pedigree: originated in Switzerland

AKC Group: Mastiff, AKC Working

Breed Size: Large

Height: average 25.5 – 27.5 inches

Weight: 110 – 200 pounds

Coat Length: can have either long or short hair

Coat Texture: fine and smooth

Shedding: sheds twice a year (spring and fall)

Color: brindle grizzle, brown and white, mahogany and white, orange and white, red and white, rust and white, white and brown, white orange, white and red

Eyes: medium-sized set to the sides, and dark in color

Nose: broad, with wide-open nostrils, black

Ears: medium-sized ears that are set high, dropping, and slightly away from the head

Tail: long, broad and powerful at the base, often held low when the dog is relaxed

Temperament: gentle, friendly, slow, patient, obedient, loyal

Strangers: generally friendly to everyone

Children: generally good with children, but (like all dogs) should be supervised around young and small children

Other Dogs: generally good with other dogs and other animals if properly trained and socialized

Training: very easy to train

Exercise Needs: needs to be exercised regularly, with long walks and short games

Health Conditions: hip dysplasia, allergies, hemi vertebrae, IDD, Elongated Soft Palate

Lifespan: 8 – 10 years

Nickname: Saint

Habitat Requirements

Recommended Accessories: crate, dog bed, fences/gates, food/water dishes, toys, leash, harness, grooming supplies

Harness: sized by weight

Grooming Supplies: organic oatmeal shampoo for dogs, rubber gloves or soft bristle brush, baby powder

Grooming Frequency: brush and bathed once needed, most probably once every 2 weeks

Energy Level: Laid back

Exercise Requirements: at least 20 minutes per day

Crate: highly recommended

Crate Size: just large enough for dog to lie down and turn around comfortably

Crate Extras: Dog Mattress

Toys: start with an assortment, see what the dog likes; include some mentally stimulating toys

Exercise Ideas: walks or indoor games

Food/Water bowls: stainless steel or ceramic bowls, clean daily

Nutritional Needs

Nutritional Needs: water, protein, carbohydrate, fats, vitamins, minerals

Restrictions: grains, soy, corn

Calorie Needs: varies by age, weight, and activity level

Amount to Feed (puppy): 2-3 cups a day

Amount to Feed (adult): 4-8 cups a day

Feeding Frequency: two to four meals daily

Important Ingredients: fresh animal protein (chicken, beef, lamb, turkey, eggs), digestible carbohydrates, animal fats

Important Minerals: calcium, phosphorus, potassium, magnesium, iron, copper and manganese

Important Vitamins: Vitamin A, Vitamin A, Vitamin B-12, Vitamin D, Vitamin C

Dog Food Brands to choose from: Blue Buffalo Life Protection Large Breed Adult Fish & Oatmeal Recipe, EVO Red Meat Formula, Large Bites Dry Food, Nature's Variety Instinct Ultimate Protein Duck Formula

Breeding Information

Age of First Heat: around 6 months (or earlier)

Heat (Estrus) Cycle: 14 to 21 days

Frequency: twice a year, every 6 to 7 months

Breeding Age: at least 2 years old

Breeding Pair: both healthy

Time between Litters: at least one heat cycle, ideally one year

Greatest Fertility: 11 to 15 days into the cycle

Gestation Period: 60 to 63 days, but can extend up to 5 more days

Pregnancy Detection: possible after 21 days, best to wait 28 days before exam

Feeding Pregnant Dogs: maintain normal diet until week 5 or 6 then slightly increase rations

Signs of Labor: body temperature drops below normal 100° to 102°F (37.7° to 38.8°C), may be as low as 98°F (36.6°C); dog begins nesting in a dark, quiet place

Contractions: period of 10 minutes in waves of 3 to 5 followed by a period of rest

Whelping: C-section

Puppies: born with eyes and ears closed; eyes open at 10-12 days, teeth develop at 4-5 weeks

Litter Size: 6 to 8 puppies

Size at Birth: about 1 ½ - 2 ½ pounds

Weaning: start offering puppy food soaked in water at 6 weeks; fully weaned by 10 weeks

Socialization: start as early as possible to prevent puppies from being nervous as an adult

First Aid Kit

In case of an emergency, all dog owners should have a first aid kit which consists of the following:

- Magnifying glass
- Scissors
- Tweezers
- Nail clippers and metal nail file
- Styptic powder
- Penlight
- Eye dropper or oral syringe
- Cotton swabs
- Cotton balls
- Clean towels – cloth and paper
- Rectal thermometer
- Lubricant such as mineral oil or Petroleum Jelly
- Disposable gloves
- Bitter Apple or other product to discourage chewing
- Pet carrier
- 2 Towels or blankets to use as a stretcher and insulator
- Cold packs and heat packs (wrap in towel before using)
- Wound disinfectant such as Betadine or Nolvasan
- Triple antibiotic ointment for skin
- Antibiotic ophthalmic ointment for eyes, e.g.,Terramycin
- Eye wash solution
- Sterile saline
- Antidiarrheal medicine

- Antihistamine for allergic reactions
- Cortisone spray to aid in itch relief
- Ear cleaning solution
- Hydrogen peroxide
- Activated charcoal to absorb ingested poisons
- Square gauze of various sizes – some sterile
- Non-stick pads
- First aid tape – both paper and adhesive types
- Bandage rolls – gauze and Vetwrap
- Band-Aids

Important Note: Before administering first aid on your dog, be sure to consult your veterinarian and ask about the important data you need.

Index

C

D

E

F

G

H

I

K

L

Photo Credits

Page 96 Photo by Localpups via Flickr
<https://www.flickr.com/photos/133374862@N02/2050303071
5/>

Page 100 Photo by Nan Palermo via Flickr
<https://flic.kr/p/qK35pk>

Page 104 Photo by Alan Morris via Flickr
<https://flic.kr/p/NqfESo >

Page 114 Photo by Gerald Ferreira via Flickr
<https://flic.kr/p/5Bh81D >

References

"AAFCO Dog Food Nutrient Profiles"
DogFoodAdvisor.com
<http://www.dogfoodadvisor.com/frequently-asked-
questions/aafco-nutrient-profiles/>

"Annual Dog Care Costs" PetFinder.com
<https://www.petfinder.com/pet-adoption/dog-
adoption/annual-dog-care-costs/>

"Choosing a Healthy Puppy" WebMD
<http://pets.webmd.com/dogs/guide/choosing-healthy-
puppy>

"How to Find a Responsible Breeder" HumaneSociety.org
<http://www.humanesociety.org/issues/puppy_mills/tips/f
inding_responsible_dog_breeder.html?referrer=https://ww
w.google.com/>

"My Bowl: What Goes into a Balanced Diet for Your Dog?"
PetMD.com
<http://www.petmd.com/dog/slideshows/
nutrition-center/my-bowl-what-goes-into-a-balanced-diet-
for-your-dog>

"Nutrients Your Dog Needs" ASPCA.org
<https://www.aspca.org/pet-care/dog-care/nutrients-your-dog-needs>

"Nutrition: General Feeding Guidelines for Dogs"
VCAAnimalHospitals.com
<http://www.vcahospitals.com/main/pet-health-information/article/animal-health/nutrition-general-feeding-guidelines-for-dogs/6491>

"Official Breed Standard of Saint Bernard" AKC.org
<www.akc.org/dog-breeds/st-bernard/>

"Pet Care Costs" ASPCA.org
<https://www.aspca.org/adopt/pet-care-costs>

"Puppy Proofing Your Home" Hill's Pet.com
<http://www.hillspet.com/dog-care/puppy-proofing-your-home.html>

"Puppy Proofing Your Home" PetEducation.com
<http://www.peteducation.com/article.cfm?c=2+2106&aid=3283>

"Saint Bernard" Vetstreet.com
<http://www.vetstreet.com/dogs/saint-bernard>

"Saint Bernard Dog Breed" Dogtime.com
<http://dogtime.com/dog-breeds/saint-bernard>

"Saint Bernard Dog Breed Information and Pictures"
DogBreedInfo.com
<http://www.dogbreedinfo.com/saintbernard.htm>

"The Saint Bernard" AKC.org
<www.akc.org/dog-breeds/st-bernard/>

"Vitamins and Minerals Your Dog Needs" Kim Boatman
TheDogDaily.com
<http://www.thedogdaily.com/dish/diet/dogs_vitamins/inde
x.html#.VHOtMPnF_IA>

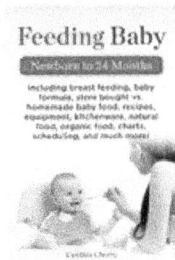

Feeding Baby
Cynthia Cherry
978-1941070000

Axolotl
Lolly Brown
978-0989658430

Dysautonomia, POTS
Syndrome
Frederick Earlstein
978-0989658485

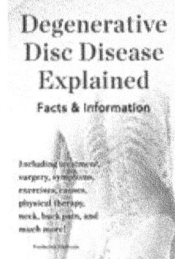

Degenerative Disc
Disease Explained
Frederick Earlstein
978-0989658485

Sinusitis, Hay Fever,
Allergic Rhinitis Explained
Frederick Earlstein
978-1941070024

Wicca
Riley Star
978-1941070130

Zombie Apocalypse
Rex Cutty
978-1941070154

Capybara
Lolly Brown
978-1941070062

Eels As Pets
Lolly Brown
978-1941070167

Scabies and Lice Explained
Frederick Earlstein
978-1941070017

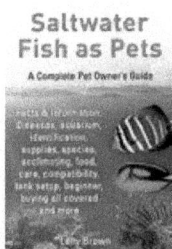

Saltwater Fish As Pets
Lolly Brown
978-0989658461

Torticollis Explained
Frederick Earlstein
978-1941070055

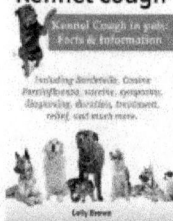

Kennel Cough
Lolly Brown
978-0989658409

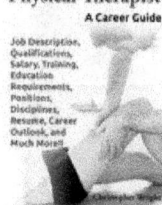

Physiotherapist, Physical
Therapist
Christopher Wright
978-0989658492

Rats, Mice, and Dormice
As Pets
Lolly Brown
978-1941070079

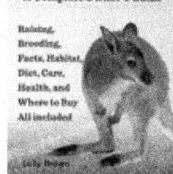

Wallaby and Wallaroo Care
Lolly Brown
978-1941070031

Bodybuilding Supplements
Explained
Jon Shelton
978-1941070239

Demonology
Riley Star
978-19401070314

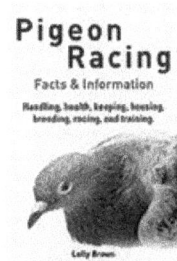

Pigeon Racing
Lolly Brown
978-1941070307

Dwarf Hamster
Lolly Brown
978-1941070390

Cryptozoology
Rex Cutty
978-1941070406

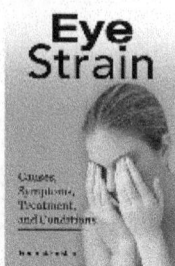

Eye Strain
Frederick Earlstein
978-1941070369

Inez The Miniature Elephant
Asher Ray
978-1941070353

Vampire Apocalypse
Rex Cutty
978-1941070321

www.ingramcontent.com/pod-product-compliance
Lightning Source LLC
Chambersburg PA
CBHW052104090426
42741CB00009B/1674